Microservices Archit

I0016690

Make the architecture of a software

as simple as possible

Edward Cambell

Disclaimer

While all attempts have been made to verify the information provided in this book, the author doesn't assume any responsibility for errors, omissions, or contrary interpretations of the subject matter contained within. **The information provided in this book is for educational and entertainment purposes only. The reader is responsible for his or her own actions and the author does not accept any responsibilities for any liabilities or damages, real or perceived, resulting from the use of this information.**

The trademarks that are used are without any consent, and the publication of the trademark is without permission or backing by the trademark owner. All trademarks and brands within this book are for clarifying purposes only and are the owned by the owners themselves, not affiliated

with this document.

Contents

This book is all about microservices architecture patterns. The book starts by explaining what microservices architecture patterns are, as well as where and how they can be developed and used. The book will guide you through various strategies for separating your application into a set of services which run either dependently or independently of one another.

Book Description

This book is all about microservices architecture patterns. The book starts by explaining what microservices architecture patterns are, as well as where and how they can be developed and used. The book will guide you through various strategies for separating your application into a set of services which run either dependently or independently of one another.

Also explained is how communication between different services of an application takes place both synchronously and asynchronously and the advantages of using microservices architectural patterns as well as the drawbacks associated with its use. Some websites which have migrated from the use of monolithic patterns to microservices patterns are also discussed.

Along with an explanation of where and how to implement them and their various advantages and disadvantages, the following topics will be discussed:

- Definition

- Monolithic Architecture

- API Gateway Microservices Architecture

- Client-side service discovery

- Server-side Service Discovery

- 3rd Party Registration

- Self Registration

- Service Registry

- Single service instances per host

- Multiple service Instances per Host

- Service Instance per VM

- Service instance per container

Introduction

Most of the software architectures in use today are very complex. We need to make the architecture of a software application as simple as possible so that the process of interaction can be made as simple as possible. This will even make it possible for non-computer experts to easily interact with these applications.

One way to achieve this is by using microservices. Using microservices breaks an application down into a set of individual components, or 'services', which are set up to communicate with one another. Communication between services can be done either synchronously or asynchronously. One should also know how to divide or decompose into services. There are various strategies on how this can be done which will be discussed later in this text.

One also needs to understand how to register the instances of a particular service with the service registry. Registration is done on starting up. After shutdown of the application, deregistration occurs, where the instances of the service are unregistered from the service registry. One can have the services register themselves in what we call self-registration or can choose to register the services manually. There exists various microservices architecture patterns. Each has its own advantages and disadvantages which will be expanded upon later.

Chapter 1:

Definition

Microservices is a computing term used to refer to a software architecture style where complex applications are made up of small, independent processes which communicate with each other using language-agnostic APIs. The services are focused on accomplishing small tasks making them easy to alter or replace and are then highly coupled and organized based on their capabilities.

Microservices architectural patterns are used to solve common problems which occur in software architectures such as performance limitation and unavailability. When compared to other software design patterns, these have a wider scope.

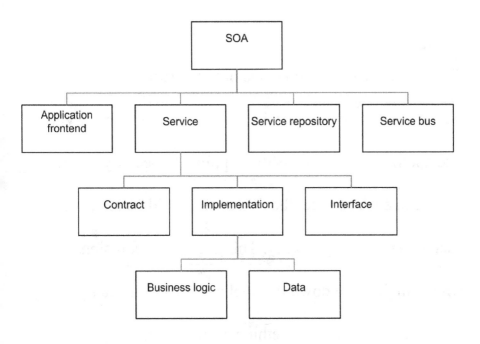

Today, there are numerous Microservices architecture patterns, which are intended to provide a high level of interactivity on the client side. Application developers expect their applications to run on cloud environments, be highly available and highly scalable. The main problem to be solved with the microservices architectural patterns is how to deploy the application so that clients are able to use it.

The solution to this problem is only to break down the whole application into services which can collaborate with one another. Scale cube is then applied, especially on the y-axis. In each service, the functions should be related to each other and very closely. This is to avoid collisions which might slow down the application. As an example a service might handle something such as managing customers or managing orders from customers. With each of these two services, the set of functions involved is highly related.

Synchronous protocols are used so that one service can communicate with another service. An example of the synchronous protocol is the HTTP/REST protocol. Asynchronous protocols, such as AMQP, on the other hand are used for communication between different services.

The process of developing different services is done independently, meaning that they are developed separately since they are intended to perform different functions. The same case applies to deployment.

Each of the services contains its own database. This makes it possible to decouple it from the set of other services and also to maintain consistency between different databases belonging to different services. This is achieved by using either application-level events or database replication mechanisms.

Using microservices patterns comes with the following benefits:

1. Microservices are very small. This makes it easier for the developers to understand them. The integrated development environment (IDE) itself is faster and this improves the developer's productivity. Since the web container takes a very short time to get started, the process of deploying the application is made much faster which also helps to increases the productivity of the developer.

2. A service can be deployed on its own without the other services. This means that new versions of a particular service can be easily deployed following its developments.

3. The process of development can be easily scaled. It is easy to organize and separate services so that

multiple teams participate in development, each working on a single service.

4. Improved isolation of faults. If, for example, there is a memory leak in one of the services, the other services can easily be protected from the effects of the memory leakage. They are free to continue with their job of handling requests from the clients. In the monolithic architecture, by comparison, if a memory leakage should occur in any of the services, then the end result will be a breakdown of the whole application.

5. Development and deployment of each service can be done independently.

6. The task of committing yourself to a long-term stack of a particular technology is avoided.

Unfortunately, it also comes with the following drawbacks:

1. Developers must create an additional distributed system, which creates more complexity. Most of the available integrated development environments (IDEs) are solely developed to help developers come up with monolithic architectures, not distributed systems. The process of testing also becomes more difficult.

2. The developer is expected to create a mechanism for services to communicate with each other. This requires coordination between different teams

working on different services which might lead to difficulties between these teams.

3. The process of deploying the application in a production environment is very complex. Notice that the application involves many services which are running. Managing these services is difficult, especially when coordination is needed.

4. Memory consumption is high. If there are K instances of an application in the monolithic architectural pattern, then the microservice architectural pattern replaces this with K*L instances of the same application. Due to the increased number of instances, the result will be increased overhead on the part of the team responsible for a particular service. If each of the

services in the application is running on its own virtual machine, then the situation will become much worse as more overhead will be experienced.

Deciding to use the microservice architectural pattern can be problematic. When developing an application for the first time, it may not seem to make sense to use this pattern. Due to the distributed architecture of this pattern, the development can be slow.

If you are just starting up, this might not be your intention, as you only need to evolve your business model and the associated application. The process of breaking down the Y-axis might lead to difficulties while iterating.

Once you get into the production environment, you will definitely need to scale. Decomposition of different functions will be needed, but due to the dependencies between the different services of the application, this might be difficult.

You will also experience a challenge when it is time to decompose your application into a set of microservices. This process is a kind of art. There are numerous strategies for achieving it. You can choose to use either a use case or a verb for this purpose. For example, shipping orders which have been completed. The login functionality can be partitioned using the verb strategy.

You can also partition the application using the noun and resources strategy. This is applicable on all the operations that can be applied on the entities or resources of a specific type. For example, when you want to keep a record of your stock. The best idea when implementing this pattern is to make it in such a way that each of the services has only a limited set of tasks. You should make use of the principle of Single responsibility, in which each of the services will be developed to accomplish only one task. A certain service can only be changed for one reason.

You can also make use of the UNIX utilities for design purpose. These include the cat, grep and find. Each of the utilities that you have used should be used to accomplish a unit task. If you want to achieve complex functionalities, combine the UNIX utilizes with the shell scripts and the effect will be amazing.

Uses

Large websites such as Amazon, eBay and Netflix use the microservices pattern rather than the monolithic pattern. Netflix offers video streaming services, meaning that the site should be able to support complex functionalities. The live streaming is also supported on multiple devices. Amazon, which initially used a two tier architecture had to change to an architecture which is service oriented so as to provide better services to its clients.

The site eBay also changed to an architecture which is services oriented. They were initially using the monolithic architecture. The tier itself is made up of multiple services which run independently from one another. The main business logic here is either to sell or to buy.

Chapter 2:

Monolithic Architecture

In this architecture, the server side components are packaged into a single unit. This is just a server-side enterprise application. 3rd parties may have an API to consume. Several types of clients must be supported by this application, including native mobile applications, mobile browsers and desktop browsers.

To integrate the application with other web applications, one can use either a message broker or web services. The application functions by processing the requests received from the clients and then servicing the request. The request can be messages or the HTTP requests.

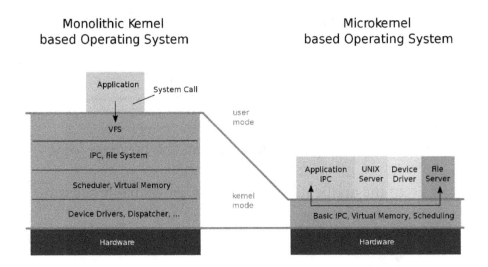

To process the request, the application can process the business logic, exchange messages with the necessary applications or access the database. The response returned is either in the form of HTML, JSON or XML.

The structure of the application can either be hexagonal or layered. It has the following components:

- Presentation components – these receive requests from the user and display the results in either

JSON, HTML or XML. This is what happens with web services.

- Business logic –this represents the business logic of the application. It is where the actual processing is done.

- Database access logic –these are the data access objects which are responsible for accessing the database.

- Application integration logic –this is the layer responsible for sending the messages based on spring integration.

Logical components exist and correspond to the different areas of the application. The problem associated with this

Microservices architecture pattern is the deployment architecture of the application.

The following forces must be involved in the development of Monolithic Microservices Architectural design pattern:

- A team of developers must work on the application.
- Members who join the team should become productive as quickly as possible.
- The application must be easily understood and modified.
- Deployment of the application must be done continuously.
- The application must be tested in terms of its availability and its ability to scale. This should be done by the running multiple versions of the application on different machines at the same time.

- You should take advantage of emerging trends in technology. These include new programming languages and features and frameworks.

Examples of applications with a monolithic architecture include a single java WAR file and a single directory hierarchy of NodeJS code or Rails.

An example of a context which is suitable for using the monolithic architectural pattern is when you want to build an e-commerce system which is supposed to take orders from customers. The application should then verify an inventory or check for availability of credit. These should then be shipped to where necessary.

You have to create a user interface which will interact with the customer and receive the input or display any necessary output. The processing itself should be implemented as a backend service and it should verify the inventory and check for the availability of credit. Maintenance of the inventory and shipping of the orders should also be implemented here. With that, the implementation of the application should have been done in a single monolithic architecture.

A web application developed with Java is made of a single WAR file running on Tomcat container or any other type of container.A Rails application is made of a single directory hierarchy which has been deployed using JRuby on Tomcat or Phusion Passenger on Apache. In order to improve availability or enable scalability, multiple instances of the application can be run simultaneously. This can be done behind a load balancer.

Benefits of a Monolithic Architecture

Monolithic architecture patterns come with the following benefits:

1. It is simple to develop- many IDEs and development tools are present and have been created for the purpose of developing monolithic applications.

2. Easy to scale- it is easy for one to scale a monolithic application. This can simply be done by running multiple instances of the application at the same time behind a load balancer.

3. Easy to deploy- to deploy a monolithic application, you only have to deploy the WAR file on the correct machine and you will be done.

However, this concept is associated with a number of problems and especially when the team and the application increase in size. These include the following:

1. The web container can be overloaded- if the application becomes too large, then it will take a longer time for it to start. This will lead to the developer taking more time while waiting for the application to start up, leading to lowered developer productivity. The process of deployment will also be impacted.

2. The IDE can be overloaded- if the code base becomes too much, then the IDE will become slow. This will lead to lowered developer productivity as well.

3. Large code base intimidates developers who are new to the team. Understanding and modifying the code might become difficult which will slow the development process. Since the module boundaries are not hard, with time, modularity will break down. The whole process will become a downward spiral since the code will drop in quality with time due to the difficulty of implementing a change in the code.

4. Difficulty of scaling the application- scaling of monolithic architecture can only be done in one dimension. To scale it, the volume of transactions must be increased and then the application should be run in multiple copies. The problem with this architecture is that it will not be able to scale even if the data increases in volume.

5. All the instances of the application which are being run will have to access the same data location. This will lead to increased traffic, high input/output operations and the efficiency of memory caching will be less effective. Memory consumption will also be at a high level. Different components of an application might need different resources. This will make it difficult for the application to scale because it is impossible to scale each component independently.

6. Difficult to scale development- monolithic architecture acts as an obstacle in the scaling of development. During the development process, it is necessary to divide the development team into groups. Each group should then focus on its own

functionality. With monolithic architecture, this is almost impossible since it doesn't allow the teams to work independently. The teams must work together during both development and redeployments. This also means that making a change to update the production is nearly impossible for the team.

7. It is necessary to commit to a technology stack for a long time- with monolithic architecture, the technology stack used in the early stages of the development process becomes quite familiar. This will make it difficult to adopt or change to a new technology. The big problem with this is that if the technology used in the application becomes obsolete, it becomes hard to change to a new technology in the market. Instead of doing it in a

simple manner, it could be that there is no other choice than to rewrite the whole application.

Chapter 3:

API Gateway Microservices Architecture

This architecture is mostly used when one wants to develop different user interfaces for the same application. A good example is when you are developing an online store. The user interface for the page containing the product details might need to be done in multiple versions. The user interfaces might include the following:

1. Javascript/HTML5 based user interface for mobile browsers and desktops. A server-side web application is used to generate HTML.

2. iPhone clients and native Android. The clients will use Rest APIs to interact with the server.

Interoperability Architecture

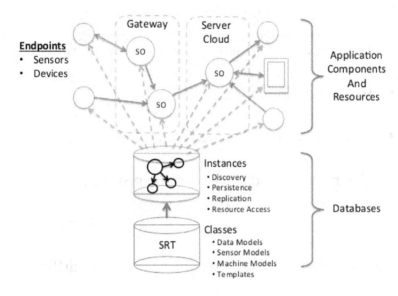

The store should provide details about the product via the Rest API so that it can be used by 3rd party applications. If the product is being sold online, then the following are some of the details that might be displayed:

- Title, owner, price and other basic information about the product.

- The purchase history of the product.

- Availability of the product.

- Other products mostly bought alongside the product.

- Buying options for the book.

- Reviews about the product from customers.

- The ranking of the seller of the product.

The details of the product must be spread over different services since the Microservices pattern is used. Examples include the following:

- Pricing service describing the price of the product.

- Product information service describing the basic information about the product.

- Inventory service describing the availability of the product.

- Order service describing how the product has been purchased.

- Review service describing the reviews about the product from customers.

If a code is used to get the details of the product, then the details must be fetched from all of these services. The problem with this architecture is on how the Microservices based application clients access individual services.

The following forces are involved in the development of this architecture:

1. Microservices usually provide APIs whose granularity is different from what is needed by the clients. Clients usually have to interact with numerous APIs since Microservices provide fine-

grained APIs. An example was given when displaying the details of a product, as information has to be fetched from numerous services.

2. Clients do not need the same data. A good example is the desktop browser and the mobile browser, the latter is less elaborate.

3. The performance of networks from different clients is different. An example is that a mobile network usually has a high latency but slow compared to other networks which do not function under mobile protocols. The network used by a mobile client is very different from the network used on the server side. This is because the client in this case is using a Wan while the server is using a LAN.

Generally, LAN is faster than WAN. This means that the web application running on the server side can make multiple requests to backend services. The mobile client can make only a few of these requests.

4. The location and number of instances of a service will keep on changing. Location in this case is the host and port.

5. Dividing into services can vary with time and it should be concealed from clients.

An API gateway whose clients have a single entry point should be implemented. Requests to the API gateway will be handled in one or two ways. Some requests are routed to several services while others are routed to the appropriate service.

Instead of using an API which fits all the clients, the API gateway can provide different API for each client. To implement security, the API gateway performs client authentication so as to be sure that it is allowed to perform a request.

This architecture is associated with the following benefits:

1. Provides an API which is optimal to the client.

2. The number of requests is greatly reduced. With this API gateway, the client is able to retrieve data from multiple services in a single trip. User experience is also improved and less overhead is experienced. API gateways are very important in mobile applications.

3. Hides the mechanism used in dividing the application into Microservices.

4. The client doesn't have to know where instances of the application are located.

5. The client is made simple since the logic responsible for calling multiple services is moved to the API gateway from the client.

The architecture is associated with the following drawbacks:

1. It is complex. The API gateway needs to be developed, deployed and then managed. This increases the level of complexity.

2. The response time will increase. This is because the API gateway creates an additional hop thus increasing the response time. However, in most applications, the delay is insignificant, so it is not a great issue.

Chapter 4:

Client-side service discovery

Services in an application will always invoke each other. In the monolithic architecture, this is achieved through procedure calls or through language-level methods. With the traditional distributed system deployment, the location of services is well known since it is fixed.

The location includes the host and the port. In this case, services can easily communicate with each other using some RPC or HTTP/REST mechanism. However, modern applications based on microservices usually run in containerized or virtualized environments. In this environments, it is hard to predict the location and the number of instances of an application since this keeps on changing. To cater for this, you must come up with a mechanism on how the clients of a particular service can send requests to dynamically changing instances of a service.

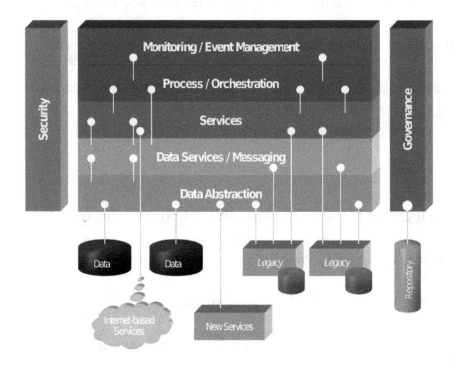

The problem with the architecture is how a client of service determines the location of an instance of a service.

The following are the forces of the architecture:

1. The location and the number of instances of a service change dynamically.

2. Each of the instances of a particular service expose an API located remotely such as the Thrift or HTTP/REST. The exposure is in terms of the host and port where the API is located.

3. Containers and virtual machines are usually given an IP address which changes dynamically. The number of instances of an application are adjusted based on the load by the EC2 Autoscaling Group.

A Service Registry is responsible for determining and knowing the location of the service. Clients who need to know the location of a particular service must begin by querying the Service Registry which Since this knows about this, it gives its response. The client will then be able to access the services of the application.

An example of client-side discovery is Netflix OSS. In this case, Eureka works as the service registry. Ribbon client is the client, and it works by first querying Eureka, which is the service registry to learn the location of the instances of the services. It is after this that it will be able to route HTTP requests to the services which are available.

The following are the benefits associated with client-side discovery:

1. It has fewer network hops and moving parts compared to the server-side discovery. This means

that the speed of the network will be a bit higher and consequently the response time.

However, client-side discovery has the following drawbacks:

1. The client and the service registry must be coupled in this pattern. This creates some form of complexity and the process is slowed.

2. Client-side service discovery has to be implemented for each framework or programming language used by the application. This creates more work and greater overhead will be experienced. An example of this is the Javascript/NodeJS and Java/Scala.

Chapter 5:

Server-side Service Discovery

Services work by calling each other. In the monolithic architecture, this is achieved via procedure calls or via language-level methods. As we said earlier, the traditional distributed system deployment works by running the services at some fixed and well known locations in terms of hosts and ports. This means that the services can easily be called via an RPC mechanism or via HTTP/REST mechanism.

Just like in the client-side discovery Microservices architecture, the number of instances of a service in this case keeps on changing dynamically. It is also hard to tell the location of any instance of a particular service. Again, our aim is to make an application that will make it possible for them to track the location of a particular instance of a service.

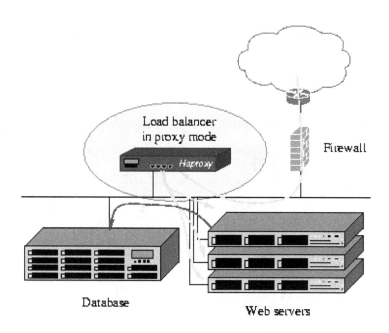

The problem which needs to be solved in this architecture is how to find the location of this dynamically changing instance of a service.

The following forces are involved:

1. The location and the number of instances of a particular service keeps on changing dynamically.

2. Each of the instances of a particular service expose an API located remotely such as the Thrift or HTTP/REST. The exposure is in terms of the host and port where the API is located.

3. Containers and virtual machines are usually given an IP address which changes dynamically. The number of instances of an application are adjusted based on the load by the EC2 Autoscaling Group.

The client starts by making a request to the load balancer, which is in most cases a router. This runs at a location which is well known by the client. Unlike in the client-side service architecture, the router is responsible for calling the service registry.

With the latter, this was directly done by the client. The service registry in this case might be located in the router. It is the one responsible for forwarding the request from the client to the instance of the service which is available.

An example of a server-side discovery is the AWS Elastic Load Balancer (ELB). The ELB receives an HTTP request from the client. It is then does load balancing of traffic on the available instances of EC2. The ELB has the ability to load balance traffic from the internet, which is the external traffic or the internal traffic from a VPC. It is also capable of working like a service registry. Registration of EC@ instances with the EC2 can be done automatically as an auto-scaling part or explicitly through a call to an API.

Marathon and Kubernetes, which are clustering methods run a proxy which works like a serve-side router on each host. For it to be able to access a service, it must use the port that has been assigned to that service and then connect to the local proxy. The proxy will then be responsible for forwarding the request from the client to the instance of the service which is available at some place in the cluster.

The following are some of the advantages of server side discovery architecture:

1. Its functionality is supported by some of the cloud environments. Example of this cloud is the AWS Elastic Load Balancer.

2. Compared to what we have in the client-side discovery, the code contained here is simpler. Clients themselves are not expected to deal with the discovery process. This is implemented in such a way that the client will only have to relay the request to the router and it is done.

The architecture is associated with the following drawbacks:

1. More hops are needed when using this architecture. This has the effect of slowing the network and increasing the response time. Although the increase might seem insignificant, it becomes significant after a long period of time.

2. One has to install and configure a router if the architecture is not part of a cloud environment. To ensure availability and capacity, one has to replicate the router. This leads to more work and overhead. More time is taken while doing all this work.

Chapter 6:

Service Registry

Clients who use a particular service usually make use of the client-side or server-side discovery mechanisms so as to be able to know the instance of the service to which they should send their request.

The problem in this case is on how the clients in a client-side discovery and routers in the server-side discovery know the instances of a service which are available.

The following forces are involved in the architecture:

1. Each of the service instances show a remote API, examples are Thrift or HTTP/REST. This is done at a particular location in terms of host and port.

2. The location and the number of instances of an application keeps on changing dynamically.

The solution to the problem is to develop a service registry, which is simply a database containing the services, their instances and the location of these instances. The instances of the service should be registered with the service registry during startup and then unregistered during shutdown. Routers and clients of a particular service query the service registry so as to know the available instances of a service.

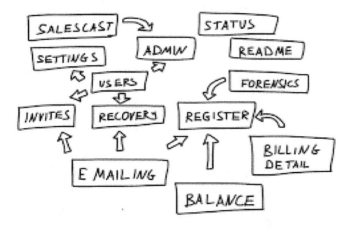

The following are examples of some of the available

service registries:

- Apache zookeeper

- Eureka

- Etcd

- Consul

The following are the benefits associated with the

service registry pattern:

1. It is possible for the routers and the clients of a particular service to discover the location of the instances of a service.

The pattern is associated with the following drawback:

1. If the registrar is not part of the infrastructure, then it must be installed since it will be seen as another component. It also needs to be configured and maintained. One also needs to ensure its availability since it is a very critical component.

The clients of a particular service needs to know the locations of the instances of the service registry. Deployment of the instances of a service registry must be done on fixed IP addresses which should also be well known. Configuration must be done with the above IP

addresses.

Chapter 7:

3rd Party Registration

Once you have used either the client-side discovery architecture or the server-side discovery architecture, you have to register the instances of a service with the service registry while starting up and then deregister while shutting down.

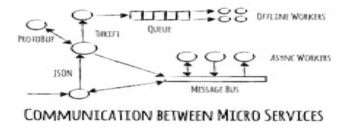

COMMUNICATION BETWEEN MICRO SERVICES

The problem to be tackled in this chapter is on how to register these service and deregister them from the service registry.

The following forces are involved:

1. The instances of a service must be registered with the service registry on startup and unregistered from the same on shutdown.

2. Any instance of a service that crashes should be immediately unregistered from the service registry.

3. If an instance of a service is running but fails or is not able to handle the requests from the clients, it should be unregistered from the service registry.

To solve this issue, a 3rd party registrar is given the task of registering and unregistering the instances of a service with the service registry. Registration of the instances of the service with the service registry is done upon startup.

When the instance of the service shuts down, then the registrar will unregister it from the service registry.

3rd party registration pattern is associated with the following benefits:

1. The code for the service is very simple in comparison to using a self-registration pattern. This is because it has no responsibility for registering itself.

2. The registrar has the ability to check the status of the instance of a service and take the necessary action based on the results of the check.

The architecture is associated with the following drawbacks:

1. If the registrar is not part of the infrastructure, then it must be installed since it will be seen as another component. It also needs to be configured and maintained. One also needs to ensure the availability of this component since it is a very critical component.

2. The registrar, which is a third party in this case might have only basic information about the instance of the service. Example, it can only know that the instance is running or not running, meaning that it will have information on whether request can be handled or not. However, some registrars have the ability to check on the status of the instance of a service.

Chapter 8:

Self Registration

As we said in the 3rd party registration chapter, the instances of a service need to be registered on startup and unregistered on shutdown.

The problem is on how to register and unregister the instances of a service with the service registry.

The following forces are involved:

1. The instances of a service must be registered with the service registry on startup and unregistered from the same on shutdown.

2. Any instance of a service that crashes should be immediately unregistered from the service registry.

3. If an instance of a service is running but fails or is not able to handle the requests from the clients, it should be unregistered from the service registry.

In this architecture, this problem is solved by each instance of a service taking the responsibility of registering itself with the service registry. Once the service is started, the instance registers itself with the service registering using the host name and the IP address.

It also makes itself available so that it can be discovered. The client does the renewal of the registration on a regular basis so that the registry can be aware that it is still alive. During shutdown, the instance of the service again takes the responsibility of unregistering itself from the service

registry.

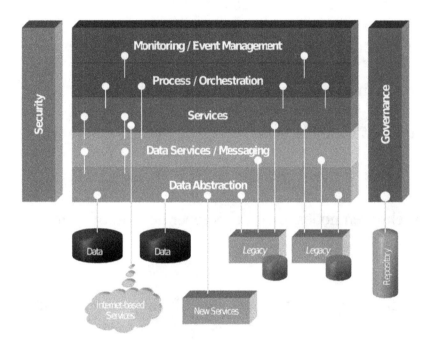

An example of a service registry is Netflix Eureka.

Instances of a service use the client API and the

registration API that it provides to register themselves.

Apache Zookeeper is another service registry. A Zookeeper znode is associated with each service. Children of the znode are created once the instance is started and these will contain the location of each of the instances. Clients then have to retrieve the children for these locations to be able to know where a particular instance of a service is. If the clients end without having gotten rid of these children nodes, then ZooKeeper gets rid of them.

The architecture is associated with the following benefit:

1. Each instance of a service knows its state very well, meaning that a state model can be implemented which will be more than the available or unavailable status.

The architecture is associated with the following drawbacks:

1. The service is coupled to the service registry.

2. If an instance of a service is running but is unable to handle requests from clients, it will be unable to unregister itself from the service registry.

3. The logic behind service registration must be implemented for each new framework or programming language used to write the services.

Chapter 9:

Single service instances per host

The system architecture has been arranged into a set of services using microservices patterns. To increase both the throughput and availability of the service, it has been deployed as a set of multiple instances.

The problem associated with this pattern is that the services can be packaged and then deployed.

The following forces are involved:

1. Services are written using multiple frameworks, languages and various versions of the frameworks.

2. Each service is run in multiple instances at the same time so as to increase the availability and throughput.

3. Each service must have the capability to be deployed and scale on its own.

4. The instances of a particular service should be separated from each other.

5. The service should be able to be developed and deployed quickly.

6. The resource used by the service such as the memory and the CPU should be easily constrained.

7. The behavior of each of the instances of a service should be monitored closely.

8. The deployment of the application should be done in the most cost-effective way possible.

To solve the problem, each instance of the service should be deployed on its own host.

The following are some of the benefits associated with this architecture:

1. The instances of a services are separated from each other.

2. Each instance of a service can only consume the resources of a host on which it was installed.

3. Conflicts due to sharing of resources or interdependence amongst various instances of a service will not be experienced.

4. Each of the various instances of a service can be easily monitored, redeployed and managed.

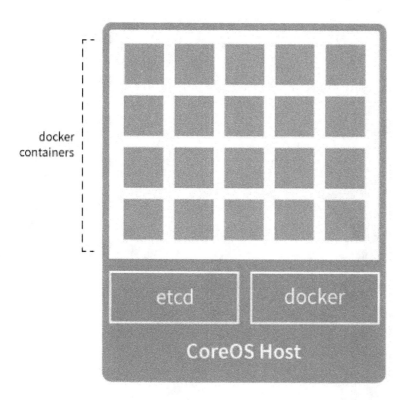

However, the architecture is associated with the following drawback:

1. Resources are not utilized efficiently since there are few hosts compared to the multiple services per host.

Chapter 10:

Multiple service Instances per Host

The system architecture has been arranged into a set of services using microservices patterns. To increase both the throughput and availability of the service, it has been deployed as a set of multiple instances.

Again, the problem here is on how to package and deploy the instances of the service.

The following forces are involved:

1. Services are written using multiple frameworks, languages and various versions of the frameworks.

2. Each service is run in multiple instances at the same time to increase the availability and throughput.

3. Each service must be able to be deployed and scaled on its own.

4. The instances of a particular service should be separated from each other.

5. The service should be developed and deployed quickly.

6. The resource used by the service such as the memory and the CPU should be easily constrained.

7. The behavior of each of the instances of a service should be monitored closely.

8. The deployment of the application should be done in the most cost-effective way possible.

To solve these problems, multiple instances of a particular service are run on different machines. The host can either be a physical or a virtual machine.

To deploy an instance of a service on a shared host, use the following methods:

1. You can deploy each of the instance of a service as a JVM process. An example is the Jetty or Tomcat instances for each instance of a service.

2. Multiple instances of the service can be deployed in the same JVM. An example is as OSGI bundles or as web applications.

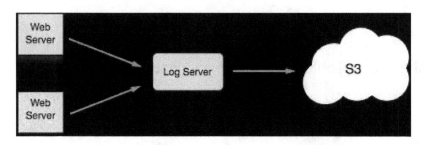

The pattern is associated with the following benefit:

1. It utilizes resources more efficiently compared to what we have in Service Instance per Host pattern.

However, the pattern is associated with the following drawbacks:

1. Since multiple instances share resources, then there can be conflicts in the requirements for these resources.

2. The versions of dependencies can also conflict due to resource sharing.

3. It is very hard to minimize the resources that an instance of a service consumes.

4. In case you deploy multiple instances of a particular resource in the same process, then it will be hard for you to monitor the kind and the amount of resources that each instance of the service consumes. Separating the instances from each other is also difficult.

Chapter 11:

Service Instance per VM

The system architecture has been arranged into a set of services using microservices patterns. To increase both the throughput and availability of the service, the service has been deployed as a set of multiple instances.

Again, the problem here is how to package and deploy the instances of the service.

The following forces are involved:

1. Services are written using multiple frameworks, languages and various versions of the frameworks.

2. Each service is run in multiple instances at the same time to increase the availability and throughput.

3. Each service must be able to be deployed and scaled on its own.

4. The instances of a particular service should be separated from each other.

5. The service should be able to be developed and deployed quickly.

6. The resource used by the service such as the memory and the CPU should be easily constrained.

7. The behavior of each of the instances of a service should be monitored closely.

8. The deployment of the application should be done in the most cost-effective way possible.

To solve the problem, the service should be packaged as a virtual machine and the each of the services should be deployed in a separate machine.

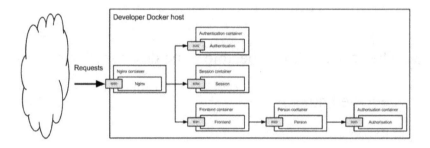

An example of this pattern is Netflix, which packages each of the services as an EC2 AMI. Each instance of a service is deployed as an EC2 instance.

The resulting architecture pattern is associated with the following benefits:

1. The process of scaling the service is straight forward since you only have to increase the instances. This can also be automatically done by you with Amazon Autoscaling Groups depending on the size of the load.

2. Each of the instances of the service is isolated.

3. The details of the technology employed to build the service are concealed. To start and stop any of the services, the procedure remains the same.

4. The amount of memory and the CPU being used by an instance of a service can be controlled or limited.

5. There are feature rich and mature infrastructures on how virtual machines can be deployed and managed

and these are provided by IaaS. Examples of these include the Autoscaling Load Balancer and the Elastic Load Balancer.

The pattern is associated with the following drawback:

1. It takes some time for one to develop a virtual machine.

Chapter 12:

Service instance per container

The system architecture has been arranged into a set of services using microservices patterns. To increase both the throughput and availability of the service, it has been deployed as a set of multiple instances.

Again, the problem here is on how to package and deploy the instances of the service.

The following forces are involved:

1. Services are written using multiple frameworks, languages and various versions of the frameworks.

2. Each service is run in multiple instances at the same time to increase the availability and throughput.

3. Each service must have the ability to be deployed and scaled on its own.

4. The instances of a particular service should be separated from each other.

5. The service should be able to be developed and deployed quickly.

6. The resource used by the service such as the memory and the CPU should be easily constrained.

7. The behavior of each of the instances of a service should be monitored closely.

8. The deployment of the application should be done in the most cost-effective way possible.

To solve these problems, the service needs to be packaged as a container image (Docker) and then each instance of the service should be deployed as a container.

The method is very popular nowadays and it has been widely used to package services. A Docker image is created after packaging the service. Each of the instances of a service becomes the Docker container.

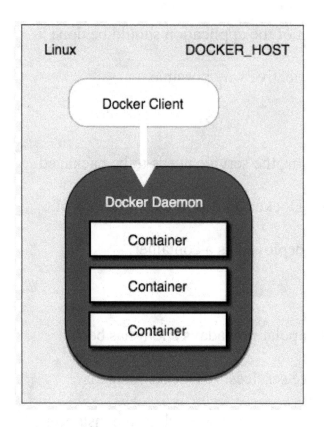

The following are some of the examples of Docker

clustering containers:

1. Mesos/Marathon.

2. Kubernetes.

3. Amazon EC2 container service.

The following are the benefits associated with this architectural pattern:

1. The process of scaling a particular service up or down is simple since you only have to change the number of instances of the service.

2. The details of the technology used in building the service is hidden in a container. The procedure for starting and stopping services is generally the same.

3. The instances of a service are separated from each other.

4. The amount of memory space or CPU used by each of the instances of a service can be limited or controlled by a container.

5. Building containers is very easy and fast. It is better to package services using the Docker rather than using AMI. The process of starting up the container is also fast. This is because you don't need to start the whole OS, only the container. This makes the whole process easy and fast.

The architecture pattern is associated with the following drawback:

1. The infrastructure provided for the installation of a container is not feature rich compared to the infrastructure provided for deployment of virtual

machine. This might make some people prefer to use the latter method compared to the containers.

As you might have noticed with this pattern, we have just refined the Service instance per host pattern. If you are unable to use this pattern, then the alternative to it is the Service instance per VM pattern.

Conclusion

Microservices is a software architecture whereby a complex task is solved by dividing the large task into processes. Several processes make up a service, meaning that a service has multiple processes. These processes are referred to as instances of a service. Several processes can communicate with each other either synchronously or asynchronously.

A team is chosen whereby each team should be focused in the development of a particular and specific service. If communication between different services of an application is needed, then the respective groups developing the services should be made to coordinate with each other during the development process so as to ensure that this happens.

Most applications are intended to get input from the user and then process this input. The processing can involve accessing a database and retrieving or changing some values, or communicating with other backend utilities. The input is received on the client side while the processing is done on the server side.

The output of the processing should also be displayed on the client side. This means that the client side of your application should be very interactive so that the process of interaction between the user and the application is made easy and faster.

There are numerous microservices architectural patterns in use today. The one to use depends on how you intend your application to function. The first step is to divide your application into a set of services where each service has its own function. There are numerous methods on how this can be achieved. To avoid propagation of faults, ensure that there are numerous dependencies between individual services. It should be easy to develop, deploy and manage each of the individual services on their own.